SARTRE IN 90 MINUTES

Sartre
IN 90 MINUTES

Paul Strathern

IVAN R. DEE
CHICAGO

Library of Congress Cataloging-in-Publication Data:
Strathern, Paul, 1940–
        Sartre in 90 minutes / Paul Strathern.
            p.   cm.—(Philosophers in 90 minutes)
        Includes bibliographical references and index.
        ISBN 1-56663-191-2 (cloth : alk. paper).—
    ISBN 1-56663-192-0 (pbk. : alk. paper)
        1. Sartre, Jean Paul, 1905–   . I. Title. II. Series.
    B2430.S34S77   1998
    194—dc21   98-13266

Contents

Introduction

Jean-Paul Sartre was the most popular philosopher in history—during his lifetime. His work was known to students, intellectuals, revolutionaries, and even the general reading public the world over.

Two main reasons account for this unprecedented popularity, neither of which has to do with Sartre's abilities as a philosopher. First, he became the spokesman for existentialism at the opportune moment—when this philosophy filled the spiritual gap left amidst the ruins of Europe, in the aftermath of World War II. And, second, his later adoption of a revolutionary stance against authority struck a chord in the era of

Che Guevara, worldwide student unrest, and sentimental sympathy for the Cultural Revolution in Communist China. Where politics was concerned, Sartre wrote about almost everything. Alas, events proved him wrong about almost everything.

Sartre's earlier philosophy is another matter. He may not have been the first existentialist, but he was the first publicly to accept this label. He was also one of its most able exponents. Sartre's ability to develop philosophical ideas, and their implications, remained unrivaled in the twentieth century. But this was done with imaginative brilliance rather than analytic rigor. As a result, he was dismissed with contempt by many orthodox thinkers, who claimed that neither he nor existentialism had anything to do with "real" philosophy.

Existentialism was the philosophy that showed the ultimate freedom of the individual, succinctly encapsulated by the night-club singer Juliette Greco: "Whatever you do, you become." Existentialism could be as shallow as this and (in the hands of Sartre) as profound as any contemporary philosophy. It was the exciting and personally involving "philosophy of action"—or, to its critics, the ultimate theory of introspection, bordering on solipsism (the belief that only I exist). Yet all are agreed that in Sartre's hands existentialism became a revolt against the European bourgeois values that lay in ruins after World War II. The bourgeoisie (essentially the middle class) came to stand for all that existentialism was not: it was impossible to be an existentialist and a bourgeois.

Sartre's Life and Works

Jean-Paul Sartre was born a bourgeois. His father was a young naval officer who died of a fever in 1906, when Sartre was one year old. Sartre was to describe this as "the greatest event of my life.... Had he lived, my father would have lain down on top of me and squashed me." Having been denied this oedipal fantasy, Sartre claimed that he grew up with no sense of filial obedience—"no super-ego . . . no aggressivity." He had no interest in authority nor any wish to exercise power over others. So it comes as something of a surprise that this saintly childhood gave rise to an undying hatred for the bourgeoisie (and any middle-class habits or values associated with this worthy section of the community), a lifelong need to combat any sort of authority, and a desire to establish psychological dominance over all who came into close contact with him. Sartre was to examine with the brilliance of genius the intricate workings of his mind, but more obvious points often eluded him.

Sartre's mother Anne-Marie, along with her saintly infant, returned home to live on the outskirts of Paris with her father Karl Schweitzer (uncle of the African missionary Albert Schweitzer). Grand-père Schweitzer was a typical French patriarchal figure of the period. He dressed in elegant suits and a Panama hat; his word was law in the otherwise entirely female household; and he was constantly unfaithful to his wife. In his autobiography *Les Mots* (*Words*), Sartre remembered him as "a handsome man with a flowing white beard who was always waiting for the next opportunity to show off. . . . He looked so much like God the Father that he was sometimes taken for him." Here surely was a superego straight out of central casting. But Sartre refused to acknowledge his grandfather in this vacant psychological role.

Young Jean-Paul and his mother were treated like the children of the household, and Sartre came to regard Anne-Marie more as a close sister than as a mother. Unlike the father figure that he claimed he didn't need, this mother-sister figure was to become an essential requirement for the rest of his life.

Judging from all descriptions, including his own, Sartre appears to have had a blissfully happy childhood. Surrounded by doting females, young Jean-Paul's ego quickly expanded to make up for its lack of a superior element. As if sanctity were not enough, the child-saint now declared to himself, "I am a genius." No one contradicted him—even grandfather swept him into his arms and called him "My little treasure!" (With characteristic obtuseness, Sartre was later to declare: "I hate my childhood and everything that survives from it.")

Unlike other conceited little brats who come to the conclusion that they are a genius, Sartre had the imagination, endurance, and exceptional mind necessary to fulfill this self-appointed role. Young Sartre was soon filling exercise book after exercise book with long tales of knightly adventure and heroism.

It was now that Sartre suffered from the accident that was to mark his appearance for life. While on a seaside vacation he caught a cold. In those days the medical profession had a respectability that far exceeded its actual ability, and the young boy's cold was allowed to develop disastrous complications. As a result, Sartre suffered from leukoma in his right eye, which led to strabismus and a partial loss of vision. In brutal unmedical language, he now had a grotesque squint, with one all-but-blind eye left in a permanent oblique stare. But solipsism can soon overcome even such blemishes, and Jean-Paul's childish idyll continued.

Then something really awful happened. His mother had the thoughtless effrontery to marry again. Jean-Paul was horrified. He was no longer the center of Anne-Marie's attention, and the new Madame Mancy moved to faraway La Rochelle with her usurper-husband Joseph. At the age of twelve, the awkward, wall-eyed child traveled to the port of La Rochelle to live with his mother and Joseph Mancy. In Sartre's autobiography (written in his fifties) his forty-three-year-old stepfather is remembered with a vividness that speaks of deep feeling. "My mother did not marry my stepfather for love ... he was not very pleasant ... a tall thin man with a black moustache ... uneven complexion ... very large nose." The authoritarian and utterly bourgeois Monsieur Mancy was ideally cast for the role of the wicked stepfather. He was rich, lived in an opulent mansion, and was an eminent citizen in a provincial city of impeccable provincial complacency. Joseph Mancy was president of the local Delaunay-Bellville shipyards. He ran his business efficiently, in old-fashioned capitalist style. (Any threat of a strike was preempted with a lockout, until hunger resolved the issue.) Every evening after work he would call his stepson into the glittering front salon where he would give him additional lessons in geometry and algebra. In keeping with his general demeanor Monsieur Mancy preferred the orthodox approach to teaching. Persistent failure to arrive at the correct answer would result in a slap.

Meanwhile the little prig in his smart Parisian knickerbockers was greeted with whistles of derision by his less fashionable fellow pupils at the *lycée*. This baptism of fire induced self-sufficiency and introversion. Sartre was not one to be cowed by bullies. His undefeated egoism developed into a full independence of mind.

The more perceptive among his classmates recognized that the short, puny dandy who had a face like a frog possessed an exceptional mind—despite the fact that he didn't excel in exams. (Possibly as a direct result of his stepfather's insistent tutoring, France's best mind of his generation usually settled about a third of the way down from the top of his class.) Sartre occupied the traditional double role of resident genius and class scapegoat. He was the unpleasant spotty little character in glasses who knew everything (and made sure everyone knew this); but he had also developed the revealing habit of making blunders. One anecdote will suffice.

(Characteristically the source is Sartre himself, forty years later.) Like all the other boys at the *lycée,* Sartre would fantasize about the women in the port's red-light district. His exceptional imagination had soon outclassed the rather paltry exploits of his teenage classmates. "I told them that there was this woman with whom I went to the hotel, that I met her in the afternoon, and that we did what they said they did with their whores. . . . I even asked my mother's maid to write me a letter: 'Dearest Jean-Paul . . . ' They guessed my trick. . . . I confessed . . . and became the laughing-stock of the class."

These were tough times. World War I had broken out, and many of Sartre's fellow pupils were living alone with their mothers, their fathers having been called to the front. The carnage in the trenches took its toll, and his bereaved classmates took out their grief-fueled aggression on anyone perceived to be in a position of weakness. Sartre developed a mental toughness as well as a certain ambivalence. He refused to conform just to join a gang of thoughtless idiots, but he longed to be accepted.

He wanted to be popular, but on his own terms. This ambivalence too would remain lifelong.

But in the privacy of his room the little frog-face with the walleye would become a prince. Seated at his desk, the boy who kept consoling himself—"I am a genius"—was already starting on the impossible task of becoming one. The exercise books filled with tales of romantic chivalry had given way to autobiographical texts. And now he began to write entire novels. By the age of fourteen he had completed his second novel, *Goetz von Berlichingen*, about a medieval German tyrant. This reaches its climax when the tyrant's subjects rise up against him, destroying the local mills and weaving shops (some of which bear more than a passing resemblance to shipyards). The tyrant is finally put to death in ingenious and excruciating fashion. His head is shoved through a hole in a steeple clock, so that it emerges at the roman numeral XII. The tyrant sweats out his last moments of life in increasing anguish as the arm of the clock rises second by second toward the point where it will decapitate him at noon.

This combination of anguish, violence, and mortal extremity were to be hallmarks of the mature writer, in whose works they retain all the immediacy of adolescent angst. The intense teenage growing pains that Sartre now experienced were to leave an indelible mark. At this age such feelings are often inextricably mixed with awakening philosophical questioning. Part of Sartre's genius was his ability to retain this combination and the emotional-intellectual force it generates in a young mind growing into awareness and bewilderment.

In 1919 Sartre began stealing money from his mother's purse. This he used to curry favor with his classmates, buying them exotic cream cakes and rum babas at a smart local café. Sartre's joy at his popularity, the sickly taste of the cakes, is undermined by guilt and uncertainty, an underlying sourness. Another poignant emotional combination that was to become a recurrent theme: sticky-sweet and nauseous.

Inevitably Sartre's ruse was unmasked, involving him in further ridicule from his ungrateful school pals and the usual parental rumpus.

16

Some sort of climax was reached, and Sartre volunteered to return to Paris, preferring to live under the iron rule of God the Grandfather rather than that of Mammon the cliché stepfather. Sartre the rebel was now learning to choose *where* to rebel: which circumstances were best suited to his particular form of rebellion—useful first steps in what was to turn into a lifelong campaign.

At fifteen Sartre became a weekly boarder at the prestigious Lycée Henri IV. He began reading voraciously, absorbing a huge range of literature, much of it beyond his emotional or intellectual comprehension. Meanwhile his writing branched out into notebooks of aphorisms and philosophical speculation. The standard of these *pensées* can be judged from his definition of love: "Desire consists of treating a woman as a means, not an end—love consists of treating a woman as an end, not a means." As with so much of this kind of quintessentially French wisdom, his remarks teetered between the spuriously epigrammatic and genuine insight. His philosophy teacher remarked perceptively of his "excessive

17

elaboration of insufficiently clarified ideas" (which remains to this day the orthodox Anglo-American position on Sartre's entire philosophy).

Sartre passed his *baccalauréat* (the tough national school graduation exam) and secured a place at the École Normale Supérieur. Contrary to its name, there is nothing normal whatsoever about this school, which skims the cream of France's university students. A selection of Sartre's contemporaries here gives an indication of the standard. These included such future stars as the philosophers Raymond Aron and Maurice Merleau-Ponty; the leading anthropologist Claude Levi-Strauss; the finest if most hysterical theologian-philosopher of her time, Simone Weil; the future great director of the École itself, Jean Hyppolyte; and the writer-philosopher Simone de Beauvoir.

Sartre thrived in this hothouse atmosphere. According to friends, his ugliness vanished the moment he spoke. The spotty little student in glasses shone at the café tables of the Left Bank. "Except when he's asleep, he *thinks* all the time." "He was the best and most generous companion imaginable. . . . Underneath the cynicism and self-disgust which he willingly displayed . . . his secret was indubitably a great softness which he managed neither to acknowledge nor to disclaim." According to Sartre himself, "I was a thousand Socrates." Emerging from his shell, he developed a prodigious thirst for beer and discovered to his delight that young women bamboozled by his intellect were capable of finding his ugliness attractive. His thirst for sexual conquests was soon second only to his thirst for beer. But neither of these could match his appetite for books, ideas, knowledge. He read *everything*—everything, it appears, except what he was required to read for his courses. To the astonishment of everyone, especially himself, Sartre failed his first attempt at the *agrégation* (graduation exam). As a result, during the following year his brilliance became a little more directional.

Despite his failure, Sartre remained the star pupil. By now he had acquired the scruffiness encouraged by student life in Paris, where running water was a rarity. Sartre soon dispensed with such bourgeois customs as bathing, and took up smoking a pipe—whose aroma was presumably strong enough to disguise any other emanating from a nearby source. He would be seen at cafés in the Latin Quarter engaged in intense intellectual discussion with his circle of cronies (which included Aron and briefly Merleau-Ponty). Philosophy was the usual topic of conversation. There was no point in joining this table unless you had something particularly intelligent to say and could say it with intellectual verve. One day the group was joined by a tall, serious-minded twenty-one-year-old girl who was interested in philosophy. Her name was Simone de Beauvoir, and she quickly demonstrated that she could hold her own in their philosophical discussions.

Simone de Beauvoir was of impeccable bourgeois background, much like Sartre. She had received an upper-class convent education, which she was now earnestly rebelling against. She quickly acquired the nickname "the Beaver"— "a symbol of hard work and energy," according to the member of the group who christened her.

(Any salacious American associations with this name would have been viewed dimly, even by Sartre's determinedly unbourgeois group, though the men were not above similar Rabelaisian witticisms when they were having a few beers on their own.)

"Charming, pretty, dresses horribly . . . she was wearing a hideous little hat," was how the debonair twenty-four-year-old Sartre assessed de Beauvoir. It was "love at first sight," according to de Beauvoir. Either way, Sartre and de Beauvoir became lovers. Sartre soon assumed the additional roles of mentor, exposer of bourgeois behavior, and clothes adviser. "From now on I'm going to take you under my wing," he told her.

It didn't quite work out that way. Despite her brilliance, he demolished her in argument. But the Beaver responded with honest and penetrating critiques of Sartre's ideas. For the first time in his life he'd met his match: the Beaver's critical pronouncements were received like holy writ. But it went deeper than this. Here was the "double" which de Beauvoir had fantasized about during the long, lonely years of her adolescence. And Sartre, far from becoming her fashion adviser, soon found himself being "mothered" (suggestions of baths, change of shirt, pimple cream, and so forth). De Beauvoir may have found her psychological double, but Sartre had also found someone who had slipped into the vacant role of sister-mother. These roles were embryonic and largely unconscious to begin with, but right from the start it was obvious that this was no casual passing relationship.

Yet there could be no question of them entering into any permanent relationship—that would have been bourgeois. Even the idea of regarding themselves as a couple was philosophically unthinkable. Bourgeois domesticity, cohabitation, "fiancé," conventional affection—such dangerous elements had to be avoided at all cost. No, theirs would be an "open" relationship, they decided. No strings attached.

The student lovers studied, ate at cheap Left Bank bistros, made love, discussed ideas in the cafés, in bed, walking in the Jardin de Luxembourg, and studied and read, and studied and read and explained, and studied again, during the hot summer weeks—and then they took their *agrégation*. When the results of the philosophy exam were posted, Sartre was first, de Beauvoir second, the cream of France's coming intellectual generation left trailing in their wake.

Cozy university days over, the student lovers now had to face the real world: teaching for de Beauvoir, military service for Sartre. In true intellectual fashion, they decided to define their relationship. Sartre stated his position: the abiding passion of his life was writing. All else would always remain secondary. Apart from writing, he believed in "travel, polygamy and transparency." After military service he had plans to become a lecturer in Japan. He wanted to preserve their special relationship but also enjoyed the company of other women. He refused to surrender his principle of personal liberty, therefore all notion of bourgeois fidelity was out. On the other hand, he did recognize that theirs *was* a special relationship. They would therefore agree to a "two-year lease." They would have two years of intimacy together, and then they would separate for two or three years. They would remain extremely close, but their relationship wouldn't grow stale and develop into a habit, like any bourgeois relationship. The two-year lease would ensure this.

Having defined their relationship in curiously bourgeois and capitalist terms, Sartre proceeded to elaborate on this in a more empathetic philosophical manner, drawing on Kant's distinction between "necessary" and "contingent" truths. For Kant, a necessary truth was one whose denial involved a self-contradiction. For example: "Philosophers seek the truth." Truth-seeking is part of the definition of a philosopher, so to deny this statement involves a self-contradiction. On the other hand, to deny the statement "Philosophers often talk twaddle" does not involve a self-contradiction. The statement is not *necessarily* true or untrue, in any logical sense. (Unless, that is, your definition of a philosopher includes the inability to talk twaddle.) The truth of the second statement is thus *contingent*.

Sartre proposed that throughout their two-year lease, and in the period after it, his relationship with the Beaver would be "necessary"; any other affairs he (or she) might embark upon would be considered "contingent." Obtuse unphilosophical thinkers may be forgiven for jumping to the wrong conclusion here. What did Sartre really mean? When he had a contingent relationship, it was not necessary—even to tell her about it? On the contrary. This was where the third element of Sartre's "travel, polygamy, transparency" life plan came into play. He wished for his relationship with de Beauvoir to be utterly clear and truthful. They would tell each other *everything* and have no secrets.

Viewed from a lifetime away, it is difficult for us to appreciate the novelty and daring of this relationship. Paris may have been the traditional city of lovers, but France in the 1920s remained in the stranglehold of bourgeois morality—as indeed did most civilized parts of the world, apart from Utah. The nuclear family was the foundation of conventional morality. Respectability was the order of the day (and hypocrisy was the order of the night). People broke the rules, but not *publicly*. Sartre and de

Beauvoir came out of the closet. This was an audacious thing to do in France at the time, and their example was later to become an inspiration to intellectuals around the world. Here was an attempt to live an honest and open relationship in which both partners were independent and free. If relationships were to be rational, this surely was the way they should be.

Whether or not even this relationship managed to achieve rationality is another matter—which will be discussed at a consequent stage of its development. Suffice to say that for the time being it did, or at least appeared to do so. In the immortal words of the man who so heroically defined the new relationship between thinking men and thinking women: "The Beaver accepted this freedom, and kept it."

Sartre set off for his eighteen-month military service, and de Beauvoir began teaching psychology at a girls' school in the Paris suburbs. Sartre must have been the worst soldier since Buster Keaton, but he eventually managed to escape into a meteorological unit, where his friend Aron was the instructor. Together they blew up weather balloons and observed them drift away across the Loire Valley. Off duty he read voraciously—again, everything, from philosophy to detective mags. In between times he would concentrate his exceptional mental powers and *think*—usually straight onto the page. The Beaver received (and sent) voluminous, almost daily letters in which they discussed the workings of their minds. And on the weekends they would meet. Sartre's invariable greeting: "I've thought up a new theory."

In fact, he was doing very much the opposite—destroying one theory after another. Descartes was wrong, Kant was inadequate, Hegel was bourgeois. Not one of the traditional philosophies was adequate to life as it was lived in the twentieth century. Intense introspection had made Sartre aware of his psychological topography, and he became fascinated by Freud. But in the end Freud too was not up to scratch: psychoanalysis denied the autonomy of the mind. As the intellectual edifices fell one by one, all that was left was the freedom of the individual.

The lecturer's job in Japan fell through, so after the army Sartre took up a teaching post at Le Havre, another provincial port city. The brilliant young student from Paris was suitably unconventional—enough to become popular with his students, but not enough to get himself the sack. One day during the holidays he was sitting drinking apricot cocktails with the Beaver and Aron at a café in Montparnasse. Sartre was expressing his dissatisfaction with philosophy—it never came to grips with real life. Aron disagreed with him: hadn't he heard of the German philosopher Husserl and phenomenology? "You see, mon petit camarade, if you're a phenomenologist, you can talk about this drink and that's philosophy." Sartre listened, spellbound. Here at last was the philosophy he had been looking for—a philosophy of the individual and his involvement in the world. Sartre applied for a grant to study Husserl, and in 1933 set off to spend a year at the French Institute in Berlin.

The overall term for the philosophy that Sartre had chosen to study was existentialism. This was originated by the nineteenth-century

Danish philosopher and religious thinker Søren Kierkegaard. He believed that the only basis for a meaningful philosophy was the "existing individual." Philosophy had nothing to do with detached contemplation of the world and the rational attempt to decipher the "truth." For Kierkegaard, truth and experience were inextricably intertwined. We had to abandon the idea that philosophy was some kind of exact science.

Previously, philosophic certainty had been based upon epistemology, which studies the grounds upon which we base our knowledge. But Kierkegaard insisted that being human meant more than thinking. We are not just reasoning minds with a body attached. Human beings are not simply, or even primarily, "knowers." They also desire, choose, act, suffer, and experience a wide range of emotions which color their experience. These too are all an integral part of experience: they are all involved in what it means to be human. This was what real philosophy should be about, according to Kierkegaard. It should be "existence philosophy" (i.e., existentialism, a word he coined).

EXISTENCE PHILOSOPHY

Kierkegaard's philosophy stressed the irrational element in human existence, thus turning all previous philosophy on its head. Typically he said: "The first thing to understand is that we do not understand." For him, subjectivity was truth. (And truth thus became subjective.) Philosophy should not aim to explain or illuminate the darkness of the world, it should aim to illuminate existence itself. We should "aspire to become this life in its complete consciousness of itself."

Here the first real difficulties of existentialism began to appear. In trying to explain itself, it became like a snake swallowing its tail. Having disavowed the rigidities of conceptual thought and argument, this left its own concepts and arguments blurred and muddied. To the rationalists, this rendered such arguments ultimately meaningless.

But Kierkegaard remained undaunted by such attacks. He continued to maintain that instead of dealing in abstract principles, we should concentrate upon the particularity of experience and its essentially individual nature. Only in this way do we come to realize our utter freedom. True, when we experience this "sentiment of the possible" it may overwhelm us with a "sense of dread" (or angst). Yet this very angst is identical with the realization of our ultimate freedom to choose our life.

The German philosopher Edmund Husserl was born in 1859, four years after the death of Kierkegaard. His work is now regarded as a development of the existentialist tradition, though he was far from being a direct follower of Kierkegaard and in fact disagreed with him on several fundamental points. Unlike Kierkegaard, Husserl retained a certain belief in traditional philosophy, at least in its aims. Indeed, his starting point was an attempt to overcome the division between the two main strands of contemporary philosophy—namely, rationalism and empiricism. The rationalist element was epitomized by its originator, the sixteenth-century Frenchman René Descartes. He based his systematic rational view of the world upon one bedrock certainty: *"Cogito ergo sum"* (I think, therefore I am).

The empiricist argument was most forcibly put by the eighteenth-century Scotsman David Hume, who maintained that we can know nothing for certain apart from what we actually experience. Even such things as causality can never be certain, for we never actually experience one thing causing another—simply a succession of events.

Husserl tried to resolve this dichotomy by seeking some fundamental level which underlay both points of view. He declared that only by analyzing the immediate experience that precedes systematic thought can we discover the philosophical ground upon which such things as logic and mathematics (i.e., the domain of reason) are based. We must return to the immediacy of reality as it presents itself to our experience. This could be done only by analyzing the raw material of consciousness, prior to the presuppositions or theories that we so habitually impose upon it. In other words, we must deal with the basic *phenomena* of our experience. To this activity, Husserl gave the name *phenomenology*.

In this way Husserl sought to turn philosophy into an exact science. Mental acts could be described in a way that freed them from our prejudices about the objective nature of the world. They could also be analyzed in such a way as to free them from assumptions about their *own* nature. Thus phenomenology would require a scrupulous and scientific examination of one's consciousness as well as of one's intellectual processes—so that one could determine the ultimate phenomena of experience and *experience it as it is.*

Now Sartre could see what Aron meant when he said that even talking about a glass of apricot cocktail could be philosophy. By examining the sticky, bilious phenomena that constituted this encounter, we could come to philosophical conclusions about the nature of experience, our being and the world, and thus existence itself. This was existentialism.

"May you live in interesting times," says the old Chinese curse. Berlin in 1933 was about as interesting as it gets. Before Sartre's arrival in September, Hitler had won election as chancellor of Germany, and during the ensuing year he set about consolidating his power—marching his storm troopers through the streets with banners and flares, holding public book burnings, dissolving the trade unions, purging the civil service and academia of Jews. Here was ideal schooling for someone who was later to set himself up as one of the leading political theorists of our time. Or so one might think. But Sartre had something far more interesting to study: his own consciousness. Judging from most reports, Sartre spent his year in Berlin in a kind of solipsistic daze, straining to discern the pure untrammeled phenomena of his experience. Meanwhile the cabarets of Isherwood and Sally Bowles were being smashed to smithereens. This lack of concern for the phenomena of *reality*—what actually went on out there, and how things worked in practice (rather than theory)—was to become a persistent feature of Sartre's philosophical activity. With regard to the epistemology and phenomenology of existentialism, this flaw remained implicit. But it was to become increasingly obvious as he developed a more political philosophy.

In 1934 Sartre returned to teach at Le Havre.

Here he began to keep a notebook of his phenomenological quest. De Beauvoir persuaded him to turn this into a novel; eventually this would be called *La Nausée* (*Nausea*). It is about a quasi-autobiographical character called Roquentin and his aimless life in provincial Bouville (Mudtown). Precious little happens, but this is perhaps the greatest portrayal of the "existential condition" ever written. It is a deeply involving work, but it is also something more—that rarest entity, a philosophical novel that is neither abstract nor didactic. In a profound sense, this is what existentialism *is*.

Sartre is nothing if not ambitious here. He poses the fundamental question: "What am I?" But he refuses to answer this in any intellectual way. For him the answer lies in describing—and brilliantly *evoking*—the very *feel* of existence.

Sartre's phenomenological quest had now led him to expand his notion of contingency. Hume had shown that we experience no such thing as causality, going on to expand his argument: "necessity is something that exists in the mind, not in objects." In other words, we *impose* it on reality. (It is an assumption, a prejudice, which may have proved vital to our evolution—but this does not mean it exists in reality.) Hume saw all this *intellectually*; Sartre's brilliance was to realize the truth of this in *experience*, i.e., existentially. *Everything was contingent.* Indeed, our entire existence was permeated with contingency. Looked at in this way, the familiar skin of cause and effect, necessity, and so forth, which cover the world, simply melts away. Take for example what happens when we look in the mirror. To begin with we see something familiar. But the longer and more profoundly we scrutinize what we see, the more unfamiliar it becomes. In the same way, this unfamiliarity can extend to our entire existence. We thus exist free from all necessity, all certainty. But as Kierkegaard had shown, this realization of the world's strangeness and contingency, and our consequent freedom in it, brings anguish—angst, dread. For Sartre-Roquentin, this manifests itself as "nausea"—which is likened to the taste of oneself, the very flavor of existence.

This phenomenological quest reaches its

climax in a celebrated passage where Roquentin confronts and "experiences" the root of a chestnut tree. In an even more profound way than one's face loses its familiarity in the mirror, for Roquentin the particularity of the chestnut tree becomes utterly alien and yet absorbing. "It no longer had the inoffensiveness of an abstract category; it was the glue of actuality, this root was molded in existence . . . the diversity of things, their individuality was only an illusion, a veneer. This veneer had melted, giving way to moist solidity, monstrous and chaotic—nude, fearfully and obscenely nude." Ultimately, reality was viscous and obscene.

During this experience Roquentin had been "nothing but awareness." And concomitant with this awareness came the realization of the utter absurdity of everything. But once again, this was no *intellectual* realization. "This absurdity was neither a mental idea nor a spoken word, but this long snake, rotting at my feet, this wooden snake [i.e., the chestnut root]. I realized that I'd found the key to existence, the key to my nausea, to my whole life. . . . I'd experienced the ab-

EXISTENCE IS OUR
ONLY 37 INDICATION
OF REALITY!

solute: the absolute or the absurd. . . . Confronting this large bulbous paw [the root], neither ignorance nor knowledge mattered: the world of explanations and reasons is not that of existence." As a result of this, Sartre understood: "Man is what he is in the present tense, and he's only there." This had important implications for those who sought meaning in their existence: "One cannot put life into perspective while living it—it steals up on you from behind and you find yourself inside it."

Sartre wrote several drafts of *La Nausée* and between times wrote a series of short stories. These are less profoundly philosophical but have a distinctly "existential" feel to them. In contrast to the novel, they depict various attempts to escape responsibility for one's own existence. The best of these is "The Wall," where a man facing death by execution tries to imagine an existence he might have lived rather than facing up to the reality of his actual existence.

Industrious as ever, Sartre also wrote directly philosophical works, in which he attempted to apply Husserl's phenomenological methods to an analysis of the emotions and the imagination. In *Sketch for a Theory of the Emotions*, the first inadequacies of the phenomenological approach become apparent. The emotions are viewed as an evasion of the phenomenological transparency that confronts existence naked. They create a "magical world" of self-delusion. In seeking a theory of the emotions, Sartre avoids a psychology of the emotions. Psychology is viewed as subordinate to philosophy rather than as an integral part of the individual. We may achieve phenomenological transparency by using our reason rather than our emotions, but its object is hardly a reasonable state. Sartre's "nothing but awareness" may have the intellect in abeyance, but the vision of viscous, obscene, nude reality is charged with emotion. Likewise the consequent brave attempt to take responsibility for our own existence, and act accordingly, can never totally elude psychological or emotional content. It may be salutory to try to act as if we are free of our psychology, but we can never completely achieve that freedom. Yet Sartre's insistence that we must never hide behind such things is undeniably a brave prescription for a philosophy of action.

By now de Beauvoir had a teaching post at nearby Rouen, and they would meet on the weekends. They also continued to correspond at length during the week. As they had intended at the outset, their relationship remained totally open. There were no secrets whatsoever between them. Yet here again this utter transparency would never be free of psychological undertones. Voyeurism and other murky elements soon became apparent. Apart from its transparency, the "necessary" relationship was not flourishing. Sartre and de Beauvoir no longer had sex, and the thirty-year-old Sartre was developing an appetite for young girls. De Beauvoir was of course aware of this. He told her *absolutely* everything, in graphic detail—which seems to have appealed to the lesbian element in de Beauvoir. Possibly to ensure that she remained in control of the situation, de Beauvoir introduced Sartre to one of her seventeen-year-old students (but only after she too had enjoyed a brief fling with her). Wanda was a waiflike half-Russian who had long blond

40

hair and an anarchic temperament (read Spinoza, barefoot in winter, etc.). Later Sartre would move on to Wanda's younger sister Olga. Throughout, Sartre and de Beauvoir retained the exemplary transparency between themselves; but where the others were concerned, a web of deceit to match any bourgeois provincial hypocrisy was soon being spun.

Sartre's other attempt at utter transparency was also not quite what it seemed. Years before even such accredited pioneers as Aldous Huxley, Sartre began experimenting with mescaline. It was under the hallucinogenic effects of this drug that he saw the vision of the chestnut tree root that he described in *La Nausée*. Whether it was mescaline or his own psychology that caused him to see ultimate reality as "viscous and obscene" is difficult to tell, and in a way irrelevant. *La Nausée* is presented as a work of fiction, and Sartre's brilliant rendition of his vision is a consummate metaphor for phenomenological transparency. (Though this was not a first. Here literature was way behind art. A quarter of a century earlier a similarly brilliant metaphorical deconstruction of our suppositions about reality had been achieved by the cubists.)

In 1937 Sartre managed to secure a teaching post in Paris and was able to return to his beloved Left Bank. Once again he could write in the cafés. This was not an affectation. The Left Bank had been the thriving Latin Quarter (student district) of Paris since well before the time of the poet François Villon in the fifteenth century. Many of the houses were centuries old and lacked even basic facilities such as stoves (for heating or cooking) and reliable plumbing. The occupants of such accommodations spent much of their time in the countless cafés and cheap restaurants that had sprung up to remedy this domestic oversight.

In April 1938 *La Nausée* was published, followed a few months later by a collection of Sartre's short stories entitled *Le Mur* (*The Wall*). Both were received with critical acclaim, establishing Sartre as the coming Left Bank literary figure. In 1939 his *Sketch for a Theory of the Emotions* was published to somewhat less acclaim, but it nonetheless added to his intellectual street-cred.

Sartre was on the brink of fame, but Europe seemed to be on the brink of war. Sartre, however, had spent a year in Berlin and knew the reality behind Hitler's aggression. "I know the state of mind of the German people; Hitler couldn't possibly dream of going to war," he assured his friends. "He's definitely bluffing." Next day Hitler invaded Poland, and the French army was mobilized. Within twenty-four hours Europe was at war and Sartre was in uniform. "The war divided my life in two," Sartre wrote later. He was to emerge from this experience completely transformed (in all but the acumen of his political judgment).

Sartre was posted to a meteorological unit at the eastern front, overlooking the Rhine Valley. The Germans could never attack here; France's eastern border with Germany was protected by the impregnable Maginot Line, the last word in modern defense. This consisted of a linear fortress of concrete bunkers and tunnels, with modern gun emplacements, stretching from Belgium to Switzerland. But the French army was not entirely modernized. One of the essential modes of communication on this front remained the carrier pigeon, and the French army reserves consisted of not a few men of the caliber of Private Sartre.

Apart from the distraction of sending up a couple of weather balloons each day, Sartre was utterly committed to his work. Unfortunately this had nothing to do with the army's work. Sartre was well into the first draft of his next novel and was busy studying Heidegger with a view to completing a "really big book" on philosophy. (The sight of a private reading a book of impenetrable German metaphysics, which even to Germans reads like a code, doesn't seem to have bothered Sartre's patriotic colleagues, or even come to the notice of his officers.)

Sartre's existentialist ideas were developing fast. In light of our contingency and thus the absurdity of our existence, we must take complete responsibility for our lives, he explained in his almost daily pages-long letters to the Beaver. We have no right to bemoan our fate. Every individual wills his own destiny: he wills his character and even the circumstances under which this character acts. Taken to its logical conclusion, this has some peculiar implications. But Sartre was never one to shirk such difficulties. Yes, this did mean that he as an individual was responsible for *everything,* he explained to the Beaver. Which meant he was even responsible for World War II. And he must be willing to accept this responsibility and act accordingly. As he later put it: "This is *my* war; it is in my image, and I deserve it . . . everything happens as if I carried the entire responsibility for this war. . . . So *I am* this war."

This seemingly ludicrous position is in fact far more defensible than many seemingly more plausible philosophical positions. (One has only to think of nihilism, or Wittgenstein's claim that all philosophy was just a misunderstanding due to linguistic errors.) As we have seen, Sartre's existentialism has its roots in both Hume's empiricism and Descartes's rationalism. Taken to their extremes, both of these veer toward lonely solipsism. (Hume: we do not actually *experience* the individual existence of others. Descartes: if everything except "I think, therefore I am" is uncertain, then the existence of others must also fall into this category.) Sartre merely grasps the bull by the horns. He shows the implications of both Descartes and Hume. It may go against all common sense (like most philosophy, and much of modern science). But if we are true to our own consciousness, and filet out all accepted prejudices and assumptions, Sartre's is a defensible position. It is also a brave one, filled with an almost Nietzschean fortitude and optimism. This is my lot—I will make the best of it. If I am free to change my life, I must be responsible for my life. We may draw the line at the multiple sclerosis sufferer or the snatched hostage forced to live chained in a dungeon, but something akin to Sartre's existential attitude informs both Stephen Hawking and several of those who survived as Beirut hostages. Such people accept what is determined in their fate and yet overcome this with their remaining freedom. They do, in one sense, take responsibility for their entire life.

Traditional philosophers object to Sartre's

position by insisting that philosophy should describe what is, not what ought to be—no matter how morally laudable this may be. But existentialism insists upon plunging philosophy into action, so it's not surprising that it should at least partly appear to be a strategy for living. (Admittedly this comes close to being morally coercive, but at this stage Sartre's idea of good was sufficiently open-ended to exclude his existentialism from the charge of being merely a system of morality in disguise. Only later, as his existentialism became more socially involved, would this change.)

Meanwhile, unaware that he was merely a pawn in the existential condition of a meteorological private in the French army, Hitler overran Belgium, outflanked the Maginot Line, and invaded France. "They have overstretched their resources and will be unable to defend such a large front," Sartre reassured de Beauvoir. But he must have changed his mind. For within a month carrier-pigeon traffic on the entire eastern front came to a halt as Private Sartre willed his, and the French army's, surrender.

Sartre was now able to travel to Germany to study Heidegger in his native land—in a prisoner-of-war camp. There conditions were no laughing matter. Even so, Sartre continued with his reading program as indefatigably as if he were still at the front line defending his native land. Heidegger held the key: it was he who had taken existentialism the next step beyond Husserl's phenomenology.

Heidegger's main work was *Sein und zeit* (*Being and Time*), published in 1927. In this he denies traditional viewpoints, such as those of Descartes and Hume. As an individual I am not, and can never be, a detached observer of the world: one whose utmost certainty is that he thinks (Descartes), or that he has experiences (Hume). No, primarily I am aware of myself as an existent being in the midst of a world. For Heidegger, my utmost certainty is my *dasein* (literally "being there," more helpfully translated as my "being-in-the-world"). Heidegger's concept of "being" is contrasted with "knowing" (through thought or experience) and the abstract concepts that arise from this knowing. Such concepts do not capture the individuality and specificity of my "being-in-the-world." This latter, and attaining a deeper awareness of it, is the business of philosophy.

Heidegger's main preoccupation is with the "question of being." In pursuit of this he even rejects Husserl's notion of phenomenology. "Acts of consciousness," free from all presuppositions, such as achieved by phenomenology, cannot be the fundamental source of our knowledge. "Being-in-the-world" remains our primary awareness, and only from this can we begin to approach "the question of the meaning of being." My fundamental sense of my own being is of course beset by the host of trivialities involved in my "being-in-the-world"—the distractions of everyday existence. But it is still possible to approach an understanding of the significance of being. How? "Only in the anticipation of death is all accidental and 'provisional' possibility driven out. . . . When one has grasped the finitude of one's existence, it pulls one away from the unending multiplicity of possibilities which immediately present themselves—

possibilities such as comfortableness, shirking, and taking things lightly. . . ." To achieve this "absolute resoluteness" we must be "free for death."

This is all very admirable, if a little Germanic. But why should we not seek out comfort, diversions, and relax a bit? Because this is not the way to understand the meaning of being, according to Heidegger. But why is such activity necessary? Or alternatively, does such activity, or even the words that describe it, have any meaning at all? This, like many other concepts Heidegger uses, remains wooly and devoid of exact definition. Indeed, the jargon he generates in trying to describe these wooly concepts often degenerates into the very "word-mysticism" he deplores. Two examples will suffice: "Temporality gets experienced in a phenomenally primordial way in Dasein's authentic Being-a-whole, in phenomenon of anticipatory resoluteness." Or: "The 'wherein' of an act of understanding which assigns or refers itself, is that for which one lets entities be encountered in the kind of Being that belongs to involvements; and this 'wherein' is the phenomenon of the world." And this is far from Heidegger at his worst.

But back to Heidegger's more intelligible arguments. For many people in early-twentieth-century Germany, Heidegger's life would have appeared to be the epitome of comfortableness, shirking, and taking things lightly. He lived the life of a university professor (complete with a well-appointed lodge in the Black Forest). His highly ambivalent attitude toward the Nazis reeked of shirking (to say the very least). And he certainly took the Nazi period lightly enough not to issue any later apology for it. But the strengths and weaknesses of Heidegger's philosophy should not be identified with the strengths and weaknesses of the man himself. At any rate, Sartre didn't—and this is what concerns us here.

Yet even taken at face value, Heidegger's arguments are not always what they seem. Underlying his earnest exhortation to shun creature comforts, face up to things, and take life seriously, are hidden assumptions which are at extreme variance with certain contemporary attitudes. For instance: in the aftermath of Nietzsche's epoch-making pronouncement "God is dead," many now believe that life itself has no overall purpose. There is no such thing as Good or Evil, and thus life has no transcendent value or meaning. In which case it is futile and can even be regarded as an absurd joke. Millions die of famine in Africa through no fault of their own; a jovial nonentity, of limited talent and ambition, becomes the most powerful man on earth. So what right do we have to claim for our own existence the privilege of utmost seriousness? Likewise, we spend much of our time "shirking"—relaxing from the hardness and suffering of existence, or facing up to ultimate questions about it. This shirking is often called enjoying yourself—which leads to happiness: the goal of right-minded philosophies from Aristotle to the present day. This enjoyment of life, or shirking, can range from reading high literature to knitting wooly socks (Heidegger's favorite hobby). And as to comfortableness: without it there would be no civilization or thought of any kind. Culture, from mathematical reasoning to operatic sentimentality or poignant penny-flute playing, requires comfortable leisure for its creation. Caught without wooly socks, having lost the key to my mountain lodge on a snowy night in the Black Forest, my thoughts do indeed turn to the "question of being"—but in a rather more practical sense than Heidegger had in mind. This is no ridiculous example. By Heidegger's criteria my frigid thoughts in the snowbound woods would have been shirking the issue. Heidegger's philosophy is just as rooted in the primacy of thought as that of Descartes.

Sartre understood this and saw it as his task to divert Heidegger's profound analysis of being from thought into action. He sought to return it to Kierkegaard's original existentialism where philosophy was concerned with subjective life—the choices and acts of the individual. But first, instead of philosophy involved in action, it was necessary for the philosopher himself to become involved in some action. Sartre was determined to get out of his prisoner-of-war camp, which he finally managed in March 1941. According to the legend, he escaped. In fact, he managed to obtain a forged medical certificate, which ensured his release and return to Paris on compassionate grounds. Had he escaped, it is unlikely the Germans would have issued him a free rail pass to Paris. And he would have been on the run with no identity documents, whereas in fact he lived quite openly, resumed his old teaching job in the suburbs, and found a room just around the corner from the Beaver. Amidst the bleak discomfort of Nazi-occupied Paris, Sartre sat down to write his philosophical masterpiece *L'Être et le néant* (*Being and Nothingness*).

This was to be no ordinary achievement. For a start, the final draft of Sartre's work occupied more than seven hundred pages. This required more paper than was easy to come by in a city beset by wartime shortages, where it was difficult to come by enough bread (consisting of chaff and sawdust)—although the café where Sartre wrote still served coffee (made with ground roasted acorns). As is evident from its title, Sartre's work was heavily influenced by Heidegger, and not just in its ideas. There are long passages in which Sartre allows his normally pellucid prose to become bogged down in a morass of jargon. Being a truly creative writer, Sartre refused to take on Heidegger's jargon wholesale and set about inventing his own impenetrable terminology. Fortunately the main message of Sartre's philosophy is radiantly clear and can be conveyed with a minimum of existentialist gobbledygook. This was to be no ordinary book of philosophy, as he explained to de Beauvoir: "There will be a few boring passages, but there will also be a few spicy ones: one concerns all holes in general, and the other focuses on the anus and love Italian style." To avoid disappointment, I had better reveal that we will be concentrating on the philosophical rather than the speleological aspects of this work.

First, an explanation of the title, *L'Être et le néant*. This delineates between human consciousness (or nothingness: *néant*) and being (or "thingness": *être*). As Sartre explained: "Consciousness . . . is total emptiness (since the entire world is outside it)." Thus consciousness is outside the realm of matter (i.e., it is "not-matter," in the jargon); and for this reason it remains beyond the realms of mechanistic determinism. It is free. Here Sartre's notion of being deviates from that of Heidegger. For Sartre, being is the conscious being of the individual who has the power to organize his awareness of the world. Husserl's phenomenology had returned consciousness to the vivid and intense awareness of artists and biblical prophets. Once again consciousness became "awe-ful, threatening, hazardous, with havens of grace and love." But Sartre goes beyond this. We do not arrive at a fundamental awareness of ourselves by simply being more profoundly conscious—as, say, in a mescaline-induced vision. No, we do this by our actions. And such choice and action takes place not in any trance of heightened awareness but in reality: "on the street, in a town, in the midst of a crowd: a thing among things, a person amongst people."

For Sartre, the fundamental is consciousness, not Heidegger's being. But consciousness cannot exist in a vacuum, it must be conscious *of something.* Here is where Sartre's philosophy becomes one of action. Unlike Heidegger, his main focus is not on the nature of being but on its two aspects. These he distinguishes as the "In-itself" (*en-soi*) and the "For-itself" (*pour-soi*). The "In-itself" is everything that is without consciousness. The "For-itself" is the nothingness, the consciousness that is free and undetermined by the world of thingness or being. Like Heidegger, this too would appear ultimately to rely upon the Cartesian certainty of thought. But Sartre dismisses the notion that his "consciousness" is thought that results in knowledge (like that of Descartes). The "For-itself" doesn't actually know anything. "The point of view of pure knowledge is contradictory; there is only the point of view of engaged knowledge." The "For-itself" is our purposive perception, which chooses and acts.

As Sartre puts it: "Consciousness chooses itself as desire." In other words, consciousness actually *creates* itself through its choices.

Sartre's entire philosophy hinges upon the freedom of the individual to choose. In doing so, he chooses himself. And this freedom remains, even when the individual finds himself in a historical situation that appears to hold him captive. Here the philosophy echoes the man, with his passionate belief in freedom and personal liberty. It also echoes the historical context. What could be more precious than freedom in a country under occupation by an enemy? Sartre's examination of, and insistence upon, the individual's ability to choose himself shows all the hallmarks of being written during the war. In this it is a brave philosophy of defiance. "If I am enlisted in a war, this is *my* war; it is in my image, and I deserve it." No mention is made of the enemy. The enemy is acceptance of the status quo, of the given—going along with the crowd rather than choosing oneself. The enemy is the acceptance of "Other," i.e., all that is other than my individual consciousness.

Yet Sartre also makes it plain that this is an absurd situation. The human enterprise—individual endeavor—is ultimately futile. There is no ultimate Good, no God, no transcendent set of values against which all are (or will be) judged. Again, the echo of living under a vicious and immoral regime is plain here. Equally obvious is that Sartre's description of the individual human

58

predicament transcends the particular conditions of Paris under Nazi occupation. Half a century later our predicament may appear less bleak and intense, but its lineaments remain identical (if we accept Sartre's atheism). Nowadays we may be inclined to a more optimistic view, but in the strict sense the human condition remains absurd and futile.

These two words were to become existentialist favorites, to the point of cliché. Among the more trivial café philosophers of the Left Bank they became a shibboleth: if you didn't consider life to be absurd and futile, you couldn't possibly be an existentialist. In light of this, it's worth examining these two key words a bit more closely. What precisely do they say about the lineaments and nature of our individual predicament? *Futile* comes from a Latin word meaning "outpouring," i.e., overflowing or leaking from a jug, to no purpose. Nowadays it tends to mean ineffectual, incapable of producing any worthwhile or lasting result. *Absurd* originally meant out of harmony and now means not conforming to reason or custom. But the English use of this word has humorous connotations which are often entirely lacking in Continental European usage. For Heidegger, the human condition was something of utmost seriousness, and even for Sartre it was no laughing matter. Ironically it is the pragmatic and humor-oriented attitude prevalent in the English-speaking world which would appear more in need of existentialism than po-faced Continental seriousness. Our "common-sense" attitude frequently tends to a shallowness devoid of philosophic content. Existentialism's attempt to delineate the individual predicament can lend a certain background depth to the wafer-thin "I" of modern Western self-understanding. Futility and absurdity can be self-enhancing as well as self-defeating.

But back to being and nothingness. The enemy is the acceptance of Other, insisted Sartre. Here Sartre was approaching the solipsism of his early attitude toward the war. Curiously he was supported in this view by his contemporary Gabriel Marcel, who was in fact the first French philosopher to embrace existentialism. In Marcel's view, as far as the individual was concerned, society "is expressible as a minus sign." Marcel was able to escape the charge of solipsism by embracing Catholicism. Sartre's individual was utterly alone. "The Other is the hidden death of my possibilities," asserted Sartre. But, as previously mentioned, consciousness is consciousness *of something.* Consciousness (nothingness) has an object (being). Sartre thus escapes the strictest solipsism, which maintains that I am the only thing that exists and the so-called outside world is merely part of my consciousness. But Sartre's position still leaves his individual consciousness very much on its own out there. In the end he is forced to resort to a convoluted argument of higher jargon. This boils down to the common-sense reasons we all accept for the existence of others in the private reverie known as our life.

Now that others have been admitted to the Other, Sartre can introduce a morality. Ironically his morality has nothing to do with others. It is a suitably absurd morality for an absurd world. With no apparent irony he maintains: "All human activities are equivalent. . . . Thus it amounts to the same thing whether one gets

61

drunk alone or is a leader of nations. If one of these activities takes precedence over the other, this will not be because of its real goal but because of the degree of consciousness which it possesses of its ideal goal." Anyone who has brought up a child, become involved with a dope addict, or felt the need to place everything on a sure thing in the Kentucky Derby will spot at once the flaw in Sartre's heroically liberal argument for the equivalence of all human activity. Yet paradoxically his ensuing argument here makes utter sense of his seemingly ludicrous earlier assertion. In choosing what we do, we should be aware of what we are doing and must take full responsibility for it. My aim should be to increase my consciousness: to become more self-aware and more aware of my predicament, as well as accepting responsibility for my predicament, my actions, and the self I create with those actions.

If there is no such thing as ultimate Good and Evil, ultimate value, then no human activity is *intrinsically* better than any other. We must accept that they are indeed all equivalent. *We* choose to make one act better than another, and we do so *by our own choice*. This boils down to the very opposite of some casual wooly liberalism where anything goes. With each choice I make I am creating not only myself but implying an entire morality *whether I like it or not*. As Sartre indicated, this should be enough to make you think. Get smashed or run for president—but be aware of what you're doing.

This brings us to one of Sartre's key concepts: *mauvais foi* (literally "bad faith," but perhaps more easily understood as "self-deception"). We act in bad faith when we delude ourselves, particularly when we attempt to rationalize human existence by imposing upon it meaning or coherence. This can be done by accepting religion or any set of given values. It also includes any acceptance of science *in so far as this attempts to impose an overall meaning on life*. To act in bad faith therefore means to avoid responsibility for one's actions by shifting this onto some outside influence.

Another key concept of Sartre's existentialism is that *existence* precedes *essence*. "This means that a human being first of all exists, encounters himself, surges up in the world—and only defines himself afterwards," according to Sartre. "There is no such thing as human nature, because there is no all-seeing God to have a conception of it. . . . A human being is nothing else but what he makes of himself; he exists only as much as he realizes himself. He is thus nothing more than the sum of his actions, nothing else but what his life is."

Sartre's explanation of human behavior inevitably falls foul of the usual psychological interpretations. One has only to consider the concept of the subconscious—its influence on our actions and its role in the formation of personality. Sartre attempted to overcome such objections by proposing his own existential psychoanalysis. In *Being and Nothingness* he uses this to interpret a variety of human actions. His main argument is as follows: "What I am is nothingness, which is an absence of being. What I long for is the being that surrounds me, which I lack. Sartre argues that our desires and the actions we take are "tributaries of this flow

64

towards being." I desire the world: I desire to possess it, and indeed to *be* it.

In a certain sense I actually become the objects I possess. Thus by possessing something, my nothingness becomes being. This echoes the process by which my nothingness becomes being in the eyes of others. More than that, it serves to protect me from this reifying infliction by giving my nothingness something to shelter behind.

Much the same thing happens when I destroy or consume something. I appropriate it and destroy its impenetrability to me. Such analysis is taken to its logical extreme with an existentialist interpretation of what happens when I smoke a cigarette (a lifelong two-packs-a-day passion of Sartre's). In his view, smoking is also an acquisitive and destructive action. My cigarette is the world: as I smoke it, I destroy it and absorb it. The fact that this may be destroying *me* is not even considered: this would be an abrogation of my responsibility for the world, presumably.

"My freedom is choosing to be God," claims Sartre, "a choice which is manifest and echoed in all my actions." *L'Être et le néant* ends with yet another convoluted argument—which character-istically appears both philosophically interesting and spurious in equal measure. "Every human reality is a passion. It attempts to lose itself in order to become being, at the same time becom-ing the In-itself which escapes contingency: the 'thing which causes itself,' which religions call God. Thus the passion of man is the opposite of the passion of Christ, for man loses himself as man so that God may be born. But the idea of God contradicts itself, and we lose ourselves in vain. Man is a useless passion."

L'Être et le néant was published in 1943 in Nazi-occupied Paris. It attracted little attention beyond those who considered themselves philo-sophers. Fortunately this latter group was (and remains) considerably larger in France than in any other country (with the exception of Ireland, where the entire population falls into this cate-gory). As a result, word soon began to spread from the few who had actually read the book to those who wished to talk about it as if they had. Existentialism, with its handy nihilistic slo-gans ("Existence is futile," "Man is a useless passion," and so forth) soon swept the Left Bank.

In 1945 World War II came to an end. The antifascist Allies were victorious in Europe, but Europe lay in ruins. The futility of this absurd situation was apparent to all. Existentialism spoke of such things in the language of now. There was no such thing as ultimate justice: millions had died, and those who survived had little else to believe in but their own individuality.

France had been humiliated and now had a need for heroes—preferably cultural (this was, after all, France). It was necessary to show that there had at least been heroic spiritual resistance to German barbarism. Picasso filled the artistic slot (despite the fact that he was Spanish), and Sartre filled the literary one (he had, after all, written a few articles for the resistance press). Under the pressure of popular acclaim, Sartre even went so far as to write a short book explaining existentialism in simple terms, called *L'Existentialism est un humanism* (translated as *Existentialism and Humanism*). Sartre and existentialism now became France's intellectual export to the world. Already the hero of the Left Bank, he now became famous among intellectuals everywhere. He even began traveling and giving talks about existentialism. The old religions had failed; this new religion of atheism and defiant despair precisely matched the mood of the time.

Juliette Greco became famous singing existentialist songs in the cellars of the Latin Quarter, and Jean-Paul Sartre sat at his table in the Café de Flore, with Simone de Beauvoir at the next table, writing his philosophy. The singer in her black outfit and the café philosopher on the Boulevard St. Germain joined the Eiffel Tower and Notre Dame among the tourist sights of Paris.

But Sartre didn't sell out. It was not in his nature to conform to anything, let alone fame and success (bourgeois concepts reeking of bad faith). He continued with his philosophical development—as ever, writing, writing, writing. Novels, plays, articles, books. And when his podgy, hopelessly unathletic body began to falter under this constant driving, he resorted to the "chemical life." Working all day every day, arguing and drinking into the early hours, Sartre kept himself going on "uppers" and "downers"—to keep his mind ticking, turn it off, wind it up again, and every now and then set off the alarm. Then the Beaver would take him on vacation, discreetly disappearing while he entertained his latest intellectually dazzled young *existentialiste*.

Sartre believed in being unpredictable. Indeed, his whole philosophy was posited on this. So it comes as something of a surprise that his philosophical development had all the unpredictability of a runaway steamroller. Beginning from an almost solipsistic individuality, it became increasingly engaged with the world, society at large, the political situation. (*Engagé* was to become another existentialist buzzword.) After the useless passion of *Being and Nothingness* and the first outreachings of existentialist psychoanalysis, existentialism flowered into a humanism.

L'Existentialism est un humanism is Sartre's clearest exposition of existentialism; within a few years this thirty-page work had been translated into every major world language. It contains the usual pithy slogans of quasi-nihilistic defiance: "We are alone, without excuses. That is what I mean when I say that man is condemned to be free." Previously Sartre had seen this freedom as gratuitous. Indeed, it seemed to encourage that notorious French concept, the *acte gratuit*: an impulsive, spontaneous action, heedless of the consequences. Fortunately this self-indulgent menace appeared more in literature than in life (for example, the character in Gide's *The Counterfeiters* who spontaneously pushes a passenger from a speeding train). Such acts, and the gratuitous existential freedom they exhibited, were said to be asocial. They showed how the true individual existed outside society, beyond its mores. (Judges tended to a similar view, ensuring that the perpetrators of such acts remained in this existential predicament for as long as possible.)

But Sartre's insistence on our gratuitous freedom was little more than his first realization of what existential freedom actually meant. It was, in a way, a purely philosophical realization. (The prewar provincial schoolmaster in Le Havre who proposed it did indulge in the occasional minor *acte gratuit*, frequently involving large amounts of beer. This made him popular with his students, but no *acte gratuit* prevented him from turning up to take his class in the morning.)

Sartre soon came to understand that although this was a tenable *philosophical* attitude, it was hardly a plausible *social* attitude. Indeed, rather than being *asocial*, as its proponents haughtily claimed, it was in fact just plain *antisocial*. In *L'Existentialism est un humanism*, Sartre's understanding of individual freedom takes on a social aspect. For Sartre, this freedom now implied social responsibility. Previously he had held that with each choice we make we are not only creating ourselves but implying an entire morality. From here it is only a small step to social responsibility. But it is a major step. It acknowledges the existence of others (rather than just Other) and accepts that these others play a distinct role in my predicament. "In choosing for himself, man chooses for all men. For in effect, of all the actions a man takes in order to create himself as he wills to be, there is not one which is not creative, at the same time, of an image such as he believes he ought to be."

"Do as you would be done by," "Peace on earth to all men of good will"—such sentiments occupy a central place in the morality of Western civilization. They received their strongest philosophical backing with Kant's categorical imperative, upon which he based his entire moral system: "Act only on that maxim whereby thou canst at the same time will that it should become a universal law." Sartre's morality was not original. It wasn't even existentialist—though he claimed it as such by setting it within the context of his own existential outlook on life and his conception of freedom.

In *L'Existentialism est un humanism* Sartre translates this humanism as follows. "Man is always outside himself: it is only by projecting and losing himself beyond himself that he makes man exist. On the other hand, by pursuing transcendent aims he himself is able to exist. Thus man is self-surpassing, and can grasp objects only in relation to his self-surpassing: he is himself the heart and center of his self-transcendence." In other words, man creates his own transcendent ideals—which may transcend the world (being) but are at the center of his *own* transcendence (nothingness). "There is no other universe except the human universe, the universe of human subjectivity."

As part of his antibourgeois attitude, Sartre had always inclined toward radical socialist views, though he insisted, "I am not a Marxist." But as his existentialism inclined toward social engagement, he found himself identifying a similar drift in philosophy itself. He concluded that there had been only three philosophies of the modern period: "that of Descartes and Locke [the forerunner of Hume], that of Kant versus Hegel, and Marxism." He soon began to see existentialism as "a parasitical system living on the margin of knowledge which at first it opposed but into which today it seeks to be integrated." In no time he was maintaining that "Marxism has reabsorbed man into the idea, and existentialism seeks him everywhere *where he is*, at his work, in his home, in the street." By 1952 Sartre had become a Marxist.

But, individualistic as ever, he refused to become a member of any political party. And, perverse as ever, his chief *bête noire* became the Communist party. "I consider that true Marxism has been completely twisted, falsified by the Communists." Previously he had been a revolutionary for philosophy; now he became a philosopher for the revolution.

Radical movements around the world took heart from his writings. He made revolutionary pronouncements on the issues of the day. In South America, in the Africa emerging from colonial rule, even in Maoist China, Sartre's books were read and his ideas debated among intellectuals. He visited Russia and Communist Eastern Europe, attempting to steer his revolutionary ideas between the rock of totalitarianism and the hard place of existential freedom. His pronouncements were used and misused by the concerned authorities and "freedom movements" to their own ends. As ever, Sartre's readings of the political situation bore little relation to political reality. Ideas remained his forte. Here indeed was a futile existence in an absurd world.

But there was undeniable bravery in the position he chose to adopt. His right-minded but simplistic stance during the Algerian War of Independence (against France) ensured that his flat was twice bombed by French right-wing extremists. On another occasion he stood alone on his soapbox outside a car factory which had been seized by the workers, delivering a speech of solidarity through his megaphone while the armed police lined up to storm the gates. Neither the police nor the workers paid any attention to his intellectual analysis of the situation. He remained essentially a one-man band of idealistic awkwardness—but through his magazine *Les Temps modernes* his voice spread across France, Europe, and the world.

Accompanied by de Beauvoir he met Castro, visited Prague *after* the Russian invasion, had tea with the commander of the Red Chinese army. Back in Paris he continued to write obsessively, driving himself on Corydane (a legally available amphetamine-based "upper"). The result was logorrhea: vast books, filled with convoluted dialectical and Marxist-inspired arguments, which never came to any conclusion.

Sartre's last important quasi-philosophical work, *Critique de la raison dialectique* (translated as *Search for a Method*), was published in 1960. In more than 750 pages he tried to work out his relationship to Marxism. "I believe that only a historical approach can explain man," he now maintained. His ideas echoed Marxist historicism, whose deterministic critique of the development of civilization and dialectical analysis of historical change appealed to his intellectual outlook. He remained a Marxist, but inevitably it had to be *his* kind of Marxism. Classical Marxism had failed to adapt to the particular circumstances of history, geography, economics, and what have you. But Sartre's main criticism of Marx himself may yet prove prophetic. In Sartre's view, Marx had not laid enough emphasis on the question of scarcity. Yet in analyzing this problem Sartre once again let his ideas run away with him. All human relationships are governed by scarcity, he maintained. Even when there appears to be overproduction, scarcity appears in the form of a scarcity of consumers. The basic rule of civilization in its present stage of development remains: "Kill or starve." Even the violence that leads to conflict is "internalized scarcity." And so forth.

Yet among all the nonsense, flashes of the old genius remained, especially in the plays he continued to write. In these the artist was better than the intellectual. The enemy, be he assassin or torturer, is often made to appear a tragic hero, trapped in a situation from which he feels there is no escape. He understands what he is doing, and is responsible for his acts, but cannot do otherwise. In the words of the leading Sartrean critic Philip Thody, such enemies "are victims of their own acts and crucified by their own intentions . . . prisoners at the bar of history and yet with no executioner but themselves." These victims are the "last representatives of a Christian sensibility in a world where God is dead but neither history nor love can take his place."

In 1964 Sartre was awarded the Nobel Prize for Literature, specifically for his autobiography of his childhood, *Les Mots* (*Words*), rather than for any of his philosophical or political writings. Inevitably he rejected the prize, insisting, "The writer must refuse to let himself be transformed by institutions."

Although suffering from increasing ill health, Sartre continued to issue intransigent political pronouncements on the events of the day in his magazine *Les Temps modernes*, and to head all manner of street demonstrations against the authorities. Right-wing extremists replied with slogans such as "Shoot Sartre!" and the police longed to lock him up, but he now had a friend at court. President de Gaulle magisterially recognized a fellow "great man of history" and let it be known: "You do not imprison Voltaire." But by this time Sartre was not so much Voltaire as Tintin. The intellectual current of the time had passed on. New ideas were emerging, such as structuralism and postmodernism—and with them new figures: Barthes, Derrida, Foucault. Pygmies in his shadow they may have been, but Paris is also the city of fashion. These were the latest intellectual fashion of the Left Bank, of "engaged" intellectuals and of the chattering classes worldwide. Sartre was old hat.

As the sixties became the seventies, Sartre increasingly paid the price for living the "chemical life"—his Faustian bargain which had enabled him to work harder than others, and live harder than others. Attended by de Beauvoir and his faithful retinue of young *existentialistes* (some of whom were by now mature women), Sartre became increasingly frail. The pills, the writing, the drinking, the smoking, the women—he had to cut down on them all in the end. On April 15, 1980, at the age of seventy-four, Sartre died. His funeral, four days later, attracted a spontaneous crowd of more than 25,000 followers as it made its way through the Latin Quarter, past the cafés where he had written his finest works. The denizens of the Left Bank, the most disrespectful audience in the world, had come to pay their last respects to the most disrespectful hero of them all.

From Sartre's Writings

Man is condemned to be free.
                    —*Existentialism and Humanism*

The world of explanations and reasons is not that of existence.
                                        —*Nausea*

The essential thing is contingency. In other words, by logical definition, existence is not necessity. To exist just means *to be there*; what exists simply appears and lets itself be *encountered*. You can never *deduce* it.
                                        —*Nausea*

The first effect of existentialism is that it puts every man in possession of himself as he is, and places the entire responsibility for his existence upon his own shoulders.

—*Existentialism and Humanism*

It is inadmissible that a man should pass judgment on Man. Existentialism does away with this sort of judgment: an existentialist will never take man as the end, since man is still to be determined.

—*Existentialism and Humanism*

Atheistic existentialism, of which I am a representative, maintains that if God doesn't exist there is at least one being whose existence comes before its essence—that is, a being which exists before it can be defined by any conception of it. That being is man—or, as Heidegger calls it, human reality.... Man first of all exists, encounters himself, surges up in the world—and defines himself afterwards.... Man is not definable, because to begin with he is nothing. He will not be anything until later, and then he will be what he makes of himself.

— *Existentialism and Humanism*

Being is the world . . . the Other. . . . *Nothingness* is the human reality, the radical negation by means of which the world is revealed. . . . Human reality is what causes this *nothingness* to be, outside *being*.

— *Being and Nothingness*

Consciousness is complete emptiness (because the entire world is outside it).

— *Being and Nothingness*

My acts cause values to spring up like partridges.

— *Being and Nothingness*

Man is a useless passion.

— *Being and Nothingness*

Hell is other people.

— *In Camera*

Chronology of Significant Philosophical Dates

6th C B.C.	The beginning of Western philosophy with Thales of Miletus.
End of 6th C B.C.	Death of Pythagoras.
399 B.C.	Socrates sentenced to death in Athens.
c 387 B.C.	Plato founds the Academy in Athens, the first university.
335 B.C.	Aristotle founds the Lyceum in Athens, a rival school to the Academy.

324 A.D.	Emperor Constantine moves capital of Roman Empire to Byzantium.
400 A.D.	St. Augustine writes his *Confessions*. Philosophy absorbed into Christian theology.
410 A.D.	Sack of Rome by Visigoths heralds opening of Dark Ages.
529 A.D.	Closure of Academy in Athens by Emperor Justinian marks end of Hellenic thought.
Mid-13th C	Thomas Aquinas writes his commentaries on Aristotle. Era of Scholasticism.
1453	Fall of Byzantium to Turks, end of Byzantine Empire.
1492	Columbus reaches America. Renaissance in Florence and revival of interest in Greek learning.
1543	Copernicus publishes *On the Revolution of the Celestial Orbs*, proving mathematically that the earth revolves around the sun.

1633	Galileo forced by church to recant heliocentric theory of the universe.
1641	Descartes publishes his *Meditations*, the start of modern philosophy.
1677	Death of Spinoza allows publication of his *Ethics*.
1687	Newton publishes *Principia*, introducing concept of gravity.
1689	Locke publishes *Essay Concerning Human Understanding*. Start of empiricism.
1710	Berkeley publishes *Principles of Human Knowledge*, advancing empiricism to new extremes.
1716	Death of Leibniz.
1739–1740	Hume publishes *Treatise of Human Nature*, taking empiricism to its logical limits.
1781	Kant, awakened from his "dogmatic slumbers" by Hume, publishes *Critique of Pure Reason*. Great era of German metaphysics begins.

1807	Hegel publishes *The Phenomenology of Mind*, high point of German metaphysics.
1818	Schopenhauer publishes *The World as Will and Representation*, introducing Indian philosophy into German metaphysics.
1889	Nietzsche, having declared "God is dead," succumbs to madness in Turin.
1921	Wittgenstein publishes *Tractatus Logico-Philosophicus*, claiming the "final solution" to the problems of philosophy.
1920s	Vienna Circle propounds Logical Positivism.
1927	Heidegger publishes *Being and Time*, heralding split between analytical and Continental philosophy.
1943	Sartre publishes *Being and Nothingness*, advancing Heidegger's thought and instigating existentialism.

1953   Posthumous publication of Wittgenstein's *Philosophical Investigations*. High era of linguistic analysis.

Chronology of Sartre's Life

1905   Jean-Paul Sartre born in Paris.

1906   Sartre's father dies.

1917   Sartre's mother marries Joseph Mancy. Sartre follows his mother and stepfather to La Rochelle.

1920   Sartre returns to Paris.

1924   Enters École Normale Supérieur.

1929   Meets Simone de Beauvoir. Finishes first in philosophy *agrégation*.

1931   Begins teaching at Le Havre.

1933   Spends year in Berlin.

1938   Publication of *La Nausée*
               (*Nausea*) brings renown.

1939   Publication of *Esquisse d'un*
               théorie des émotions (*Sketch for a*
               Theory of the Emotions), his first
               mature philosophical work.
               Outbreak of World War II, for
               which Sartre is responsible. Sartre
               called up and serves in
               meteorological unit.

1940–1941   Prisoner-of-war.

1943   Publication of *L'Être et le néant*
               (*Being and Nothingness*), his
               major philosophical work.

1944   Starts magazine *Les Temps*
               modernes.

1945   Publication of *L'Existentialism est*
               un humanism (*Existentialism and*
               Humanism). End of the war and
               period of increasing fame begins
               for Sartre as leading exponent of
               existentialism.

1952   Becomes a Marxist.

1960   Publication of *Critique de la*

	raison dialectique (translated as *Search for a Method*).
1964	Publication of autobiography *Les Mots* (*Words*). Turns down Nobel Prize.
1980	Death of Sartre in Paris, aged seventy-four. Funeral becomes a public demonstration.

Recommended Reading

Annie Cohen-Solal, *Sartre, 1905–1980* (Schoenhof)

Ronald Hayman, *Sartre: A Biography* (Carroll and Graf, 1992)

Jean-Paul Sartre, *Being and Nothingness*, trans. Hazel E. Barnes (Pocket Books, 1993)

Jean-Paul Sartre, *Existentialism and Human Emotions* (Carol Publishing Group, 1971)

Jean-Paul Sartre, *Nausea*, trans. Lloyd Alexander (New Directions, 1959)

Jean-Paul Sartre, *The Words* (Vintage Books, 1981)

Index

A NOTE ON THE AUTHOR

Paul Strathern has lectured in philosophy and mathematics and now lives and writes in London. A Somerset Maugham prize winner, he is also the author of books on history and travel as well as five novels. His articles have appeared in a great many publications, including the *Observer* (London) and the *Irish Times*. His own degree in philosophy was earned at Trinity College, Dublin.

NOW PUBLISHED IN THIS SERIES:

St. Augustine in 90 Minutes
Thomas Aquinas in 90 Minutes
Aristotle in 90 Minutes
Descartes in 90 Minutes
Hegel in 90 Minutes
Kant in 90 Minutes
Kierkegaard in 90 Minutes
Nietzsche in 90 Minutes
Plato in 90 Minutes
Sartre in 90 Minutes
Socrates in 90 Minutes
Wittgenstein in 90 Minutes

IN PREPARATION:

Bacon, Berkeley, Confucius, Hume, Leibniz, Locke, Machiavelli, Marx, J. S. Mill, Bertrand Russell, Schopenhauer, Spinoza